M000028116

ADVENT MEDITATIONS

ADVENT MEDITATIONS

Helps to 'Wait in Joyful Hope'

REVEREND PETER STRAVINSKAS

NEWMAN HOUSE PRESS
Mount Pocono   Pennsylvania

Cover art: *The Expectant Madonna with Saint Joseph*
oil and tempera on panel, French, 15th century
National Gallery of Art, Washington, D.C.
Used with permission

Published by Newman House Press
21 Fairview Avenue, Mount Pocono PA 18344

ISBN 0–9704022–1–X

Text composed in Palatino and Felix Titling
COMPOSITION BY SHORELINE GRAPHICS, ROCKLAND, MAINE
PRINTED IN THE UNITED STATES OF AMERICA

CONTENTS

WEEK THREE OF ADVENT

WEEK FOUR OF ADVENT

PREFACE

The older I get, the more I appreciate the Season of Advent. While youth is impatient and finds waiting difficult, maturity and old age grow accustomed to waiting, especially since we seem to learn the truth of the adage that "all good things come to those who wait."

No thing and no one could be more worth the wait than Jesus Christ. With minds and hearts fixed on God's holy Word, Christians do just that—and in a preeminent manner in the liturgical assembly as we experience the enfleshment of that Word during the offering of the Lord's Eucharist. That, in turn, prepares us for the beatific vision as we are granted glimpses of the glory yet to be revealed in all its fullness.

To that end, I wished to share with you my reflections on the liturgical readings for Advent in the expectation that they will spur you on to thoughts of your own. In fact, each page includes space where you can note the fruit of your own reflection.

May you expect the Word to become Flesh for you in each celebration of the Eucharistic Sacrifice, in ways every bit as real as He did in the womb of the Blessed Virgin Mary some two thousand years ago, inspiring you to echo the final words of the Book of Revelation, "Come, Lord Jesus."

WEEK ONE OF
ADVENT

FIRST SUNDAY

YEAR A

Isaiah 2:1–5
Psalms 122:1–2, 3–4a, (4b–5, 6–7), 8–9
Romans 13:11–14
Matthew 24:37–44

"Stay awake! . . . You must be prepared." The Church takes these words of Jesus as her theme for the Advent season, as believers look to three different phases of the coming of God's Kingdom among men: the birth of the Messiah, which inaugurated the Kingdom; the fulfillment of the Kingdom when Christ comes as Judge of the universe; the maintenance of Christians in the faith and love of the Kingdom through their encounters with the Lord of the sacraments. But that still leaves unanswered the basic question: Just what is this Kingdom?

Isaiah, the Church's particular voice for Advent, sums up the Kingdom in appealing images of universal and lasting peace—not unlike, it would seem, the vision of those who engage in secular peace-marches, with their placards and speeches and music. Well, not quite. Conspicuously absent from the thousands of words spoken on most of those occasions are the key words of Isaiah's prophecy: "Come, let us climb the Lord's mountain, *that* He may instruct us in His ways and we may walk in His paths." Ah, you mean there is a connection between peace, divine instruction and human obedience? You bet there is! World peace is only wishful thinking until we heed Paul's advice to "cast off deeds of darkness and put on the armor of light." Lest the Apostle to the Gentiles be accused of employing vague concepts leading to questions about what might be classified as "deeds of darkness," he lists them: carousing, drunkenness, sexual excess, lust, quarreling, jealousy. These sins keep God at bay and, by that very fact, obviate the possibility of peaceable relations in the human family.

God intends that His Kingdom be established in glory—with or without human cooperation. Hence, Jesus warns that "the coming of the Son of Man will repeat what happened in Noah's time," that is, the annihilation of evil and evildoers. Most people before the Flood, like many in our midst today (including some so-called Christians), "were totally unconcerned until the flood came and destroyed them."

As committed followers of Christ, we know with the certitude of faith that what God wills is what ultimately will be done. It is for us, then, to use this Advent in such a way that, if we cannot convince the world to "put on the armor of light" so as to experience Isaiah's vision of peace, at least we will have that peace ourselves. That peace is received from and sustained by staying in the ark of the Church, which brings us safely to the fullness of the Kingdom prepared for those who take seriously the Lord's admonition to "stay awake!"

FIRST SUNDAY

YEAR B

Isaiah 63:16b–17; 64:1, 3b–8
Psalms 80:1ac and 2b, 14–15, 17–18
1 Corinthians 1:3–9
Mark 13:33–37

Advent can be a crazy time of year if one "buys into" the current system of materialism. It can also be simply a sentimental religious exercise if we throw ourselves back to our childhood and pretend we are waiting for the birth of Baby Jesus, but Advent should be a much deeper experience than those alternatives.

As a boy, I used to hear Bishop Fulton Sheen talking about the Cross of Jesus always being in the shadows, even at Bethlehem. I used to think that the Cross was too morose a symbol to connect with the pre-Christmas celebration. But what Bishop Sheen was trying to say was that Jesus' life formed a unity, and that we cannot separate it into parts to suit our moods or whims.

I think that is one of the reasons why the Church is very careful in her selection of readings on this First Sunday of Advent, lest we get the wrong idea about this season. Notice: We don't begin with the Annunciation or even with John the Baptist; we begin with Jesus warning the people about the end of time. And this warning is what leads up to the whole point of the Advent season. We are really celebrating three different comings of

Christ during these four weeks. The first is His historical coming among us as a man some two thousand years ago. The second is His continual coming to us in the Church's sacraments. The third is His coming at the end of time as Judge.

In the Gospel reading, Jesus encourages His disciples to be vigilant and prepared for that great and glorious day when He will come again. In other words, we who live in the time between His two comings have a job to do. It is similar to the story told of the young European couple who were deeply in love; however, the young man had to go to the New World and leave his fiancée for several months. At his departure, he asked her to do something during his absence—to keep a fire going on the shore every night and to sing his favorite song. In this way, on his return, he would know in advance of her faithfulness and then take her back to the New World with him.

As Jesus left this world, He gave His disciples some things to be done. First, He asked them to love one another because of Him. Second, He asked them to celebrate the Eucharist in His memory. Because we love the Lord, we do as He commanded us, and we hope that on His return, He will find us prepared to be taken into His Kingdom.

During Advent, then, the Church invites us to see if we have been making the right kind of preparations for the Lord's coming, not only as the Babe of Bethlehem, but as the Lord of the sacraments and the Lord of the Universe. As we wait, we prepare—and that is what our prayer means when we say that "we wait in joyful hope for the coming of our Savior Jesus Christ." If the Church were to adopt the language of Madison Avenue, she would say today, "Only x more days of preparation till Christmas."

FIRST SUNDAY

YEAR C

Jeremiah 33:14–16
Psalms 25:4–5ab, 8–9, 10–14
1 Thessalonians 3:12–4:2
Luke 21:25–28, 34–36

Wake up; then stay awake. That seems to be the point the Church would have us take from the Scriptures of this first Sunday of the new liturgical year.

First, wake up! St. Paul repeatedly reminded his converts around the world that they were different from the pagans around whom and among whom they lived. At least they were supposed to be different. He encourages them to "live honorably," that is, in keeping with their Christian vocation. If Paul watched our television programs and commercials today, what would he find being advocated? Precisely the things he condemns. Then we wonder why our young people are so confused, so disoriented, for they are forced into a schizophrenic kind of existence—torn between what the world presents as a "meaningful" style of life and what Christ presents as the only valid style of life.

The movie *All the Right Moves* (1983) portrays the dilemma of young Catholics graphically. Apparently *these* Catholic teenagers (we see rosaries and crucifixes and medals all around them) live just like all the other kids in the local government high school. They fornicate; they

16

get drunk; they plot and scheme to get ahead. In fact, if they weren't shown with the external symbols of our faith, we couldn't tell these young people from the pagan Romans of Paul's day. So there is the need to wake up to the inconsistencies of one's life and to bridge the gap between what we *say* we believe and what we *do*. That's what Paul means by "living honorably."

Having been awakened to how a Christian should live, one must then stay awake. Eternal vigilance and perseverance are the keys to success in the living of a life of faith. Jesus gives the rationale for this kind of behavior: We are people destined for judgment. Our preparation for *that* day is the daily living out of a "yes" to Isaiah's invitation: "Come, let us walk in the light of the Lord!" Walking in the light of the Lord automatically saves us from walking in the darkness of this world and its perverted values. That is why the believer can never be completely at home in this world. That is why we must pray most fervently the words of today's Opening Prayer: "Increase our strength of will for doing good that Christ may find an eager welcome at His coming." Fidelity and perseverance now will be rewarded with the vision of Christ for all eternity, our faith tells us.

Secular society has latched onto all kinds of peace movements, and even total atheists find Isaiah's vision of peace beautiful and compelling. What they fail to grasp, however, is that peace in the world will never come about until a more basic peace is established: a man's peace with his God. And that comes from doing things God's way rather than our own. Until such peace is considered a national and universal priority, Isaiah's vision will be merely a pipedream, and the armies of the United Nations will continue having to stomp out major and minor conflagrations all over the earth. The song puts it tritely but correctly: "Let there be peace on earth, and let it begin with *me*." For us, that involves the acceptance of Jesus' code of life and the rejection of the world's.

At the beginning of this new year, why is the Church so preoccupied with the end of time? Because the end also marks the beginning. Salvation and damnation hang in the balance and are dependent on the choices we make and on how well we cooperate with divine grace. Our actions today have eternal consequences, so the message bears repeating: Wake up; then stay awake.

MONDAY

WEEK I

Isaiah 2:1–5 [in Year A, Isaiah 4:2–6]
Psalms 122:1–2, 3–4a, (4b–5, 6–7), 8–9
Matthew 8:5–11

Preparation is the key to the making of a good Advent. Two notions emerge from today's readings. First, for God to come among His people, mankind must establish peace, a profound harmony in which neighbor is at one with neighbor and man is on intimate terms with God. Second, God is involved in this process. The centurion makes a request, and Jesus commits Himself to action. Advent, then, is a time to ready our hearts for the meeting between God and His people by cooperating with God's plan and so be ready to share in the banquet of the Kingdom when Jesus comes again.

TUESDAY

WEEK I

Isaiah 11:1–10
Psalms 72:1–2, 7–8, 12–13, 17
Luke 10:21–24

Once again Isaiah presents us with the image of universal peace, so appealing to war-weary hearts. And though we find ourselves lapsing into a fond hope for such a day, our sophisticated modernity intervenes and we remind ourselves that wolves always devour lambs—so why bother to hope or to pray?

However, children, who are rarely among "the learned and the clever," don't *know* that Isaiah's dream is impossible, so they continue to hope and to pray. There is a side to their innocence which is naïveté, but another side of their innocence involves sinlessness, or purity of heart, or non-manipulation of others. Therefore they can teach us valuable lessons of how to bring about a kingdom of peace, based on justice.

WEDNESDAY

WEEK I

Isaiah 5:6–10a
Psalms 23:1–3a, 3b–4, 5,6
Matthew 15:29–37

Today we behold a vision of the coming kingdom in very human terms: A rich banquet, unity of peoples, physical wholeness, everlasting peace. However, it is not we who are responsible for its definitive arrival; God is. Perhaps that is why we have such difficulty in experiencing the Kingdom on earth—because we are looking for it to be accomplished by human technology (whether of secular or ecclesiastical design). No, it is God's gift for those few people who have trained their vision in accord with God's and so truly believe that the miracle of the Kingdom can indeed happen.

THURSDAY

WEEK I

Isaiah 26:1–6
Psalms 118:1 and 8–9, 19–21, 25–27ab
Matthew 7:21, 24–27

A nation which is faithful, just and trusting in the Lord is presented as the one which is God's kind of people. If our country finds little genuine joy and wonder during this season (suicides actually increase at this time of year, we are told), it may be because we have lost the virtues extolled by Isaiah and have replaced them with a confidence in the power of the dollar and expensive gifts to make others happy.

Jesus will give the gift of joy to those who are willing to go through the agony of conversion (a true change of heart) and not merely the externals of a preparation which is but a shallow cry of "Lord, Lord."

FRIDAY

WEEK I

Isaiah 29:17–24
Psalms 27:1, 4, 13–14
Matthew 9:27–31

During this season our minds are often focused on getting the right gift for the right person. What about the right gift *from* the right person? For example, have you thought about asking the Lord for a Christmas gift?

In line with today's readings, I intend to ask for understanding and sight, which produce insight. And I am confident that Almighty God will grant this request because it is asking *for* the right gift *from* the right Person.

SATURDAY

WEEK I

Isaiah 30:19–21, 23–26
Psalms 147:1–2, 3–4, 5–6
Matthew 9:35 — 10:1, 5a, 6–8

God's desire to establish the Kingdom is more for our benefit than for His. To us are given the honor and the obligation of being God's co-workers in this task of curing the sick, raising the dead and expelling demons. Do we see these as personal responsibilities, or do we prefer to slough these off onto the Church or even the government?

By the end of Advent, let's try to say that each of us has touched at least one person and cured him or her, so that person will then be one fit for the Kingdom.

THE IMMACULATE CONCEPTION

SOLEMNITY / DECEMBER 8

Genesis 3:9–15, 20
Psalms 98:1, 2–3ab, 3cd–4
Ephesians 1:3–6, 11–12
Luke 1:26–38

Many Catholics misunderstand the meaning of today's feast. They confuse the Immaculate Conception of Mary with the virginal conception of Jesus. Today's feast celebrates the fact that Mary was sinless from the very first moment of her existence. This doctrine of our Faith is extremely important because it demonstrates the care with which God guided the entire process of our salvation.

It is not a sheer accident that the Church celebrates this feast right at the outset of Advent. No, this privilege accorded to Mary was all a part of the work of salvation begun at the very moment when sin itself first entered the world. The experience of sin and its reign in our world came because of human weakness and pride. Just as a woman made possible the first sin, so too a woman made possible the work of our salvation. Mary was God's answer to Eve. Advent is a month-long celebration of God's efforts to return mankind to His favor. Mary's own immaculate (sinless) conception marked a high-water point in God's proximate preparations for the coming of the Savior.

Christians today and throughout the ages love Mary because she embodies, literally, all that we hope to be. That is why the poet Wordsworth referred to her as "our tainted nature's solitary boast." By her faith and willingness to cooperate with God, Mary showed herself to be a true daughter of Abraham. Mary further demonstrated that genuine liberation consists not in doing one's own thing as much as it consists in doing God's thing. She proved the angel right, that the Lord was truly with her, as she pronounced that fearful but firm "yes" which reversed every previous "no" in history.

Mary, the Immaculate One, said, "Let it be done to me as you say." What was the result? "The Word became flesh." Every time we imitate her response of love, God takes on flesh and comes among us once again. And that ability to say "yes" to God's plan for us is at the heart of what it means to be a son or daughter of Mary—that sinless woman who brought to life mankind's four-thousand-year-long dream for a Christmas Day.

WEEK TWO OF ADVENT

SECOND SUNDAY

YEAR A

Isaiah 11:1–10
Psalms 72:1–2, 7–8, 12–13, 17
Romans 15:4–9
Matthew 3:1–12

Advent is a season of hope, but a hope based on reality, which corresponds to the truth of Who God is and who we are. Any other kind of "hope" is false hope and thus harmful, both spiritually and psychologically—really one and the same thing if we are dealing with a healthy spirituality and a valid psychology. In the final analysis, self-deception is so cruel because it cheats people of reality now—and often also for eternity. It is against this background that Our Lord's statement today makes sense: "Give some evidence that you mean to reform." Jesus will allow for no game-playing and hence has rather harsh words for those committed to any such activity.

Protestants frequently accuse us Catholics of plugging into "cheap grace," by which they mean a less than honest and wholehearted attempt to change our lives. Too often they are right about us. How should we deal with that charge? By seeking out and accepting only "costly grace." The font of grace available to us cost Jesus His life. Should it cost us anything less?

We "give evidence that [we] mean to reform" by endeavoring to live a virtuous life, by responding to the promptings of the Holy Spirit, Who came to us in Baptism and then sealed that relationship by granting us His sevenfold gifts in Confirmation. Responding positively to the Holy Spirit automatically means responding negatively to Satan, the world, and the flesh. If "Jesus is Lord" is anything more than idle banter, He must be Lord of every aspect of our lives or Lord of none; we cannot harbor areas "safe" from His Lordship, whether it be gambling, excessive drinking, artificial contraception, or a host of other actions that seem to claim the legitimacy of a Lordship divided more or less equally between Satan and Christ. The Kingdom we await makes no provision for divided loyalties.

Evidence of reform comes when we are willing to declare our sinfulness, humbly confess those sins to another man who represents Christ to us, and then promise (and mean) that we intend never to do these things again. Going to confession without this mind-set makes a mockery of the Sacrament of Penance, and that's what non-Catholics are thinking about when they speak of "cheap grace." Steering clear of the Sacrament altogether because "I *know* I'll do it all again" is just as wrong because it is self-defeating and questioning of God's will (and power) to save. That is a denial of grace. Accepting only costly grace is the answer that leads to union with the Lord, Who inaugurates and consummates His Kingdom in the whole world and in us as individuals.

A life in the Spirit is a demanding one—and a rewarding one—not only when we slip past the gates of hell, but even right now. The reward is the recognition that our lives "glorify God, the Father of our Lord Jesus Christ."

This holy season calls us to fix our gaze on the end of time when Jesus' messianic mission is fulfilled in us. The clear message of today's Scriptures is that, at the end of time, the salvation promised and earned for us by Christ is applied to those who have demonstrated that they know what the Kingdom is all about, for they were living a Kingdom life all along.

SECOND SUNDAY

YEAR B

Isaiah 40:1–5, 9–11
Psalms 85:8ab and 9, 10–11, 12–13
2 Peter 3:8–14
Mark 1:1–8

The figure of John the Baptist looms large over the Advent season. From childhood, we have been accustomed to speak of him as a prophet. But do we understand what a prophet is?

Most people think of a prophet as a religious fortuneteller, but that is not what the biblical prophets were. They were men specially chosen by God to proclaim His message; in other words, they were—and are—His spokesmen, commissioned to preach to the people God's word of judgment about their conduct. And the prophetic mission was therefore a rather unpopular one.

John the Baptist had a task similar to that of Isaiah, who had to advise the people that God was not pleased with their behavior. Isaiah then encouraged them to change their lives, or else face the disaster that would befall them as a nation. They did not listen, and they found themselves in exile in Babylon. Once they paid for their sins, Isaiah could then announce that a day of release and hope was in the offing. During Advent, the Church puts on the prophetic mantle of Isaiah and John the Baptist; she encourages us, in the words of today's

Opening Prayer, to "remove the things that hinder us from receiving Christ with joy." What needs to be removed? An undue attachment to material things; an obsession with sex and violence; a desire to make others into copies of ourselves; a refusal to give unless we can count on a return.

These failures of ours to respond to Christ's call to perfection, believe it or not, delay the coming of His Kingdom—a kingdom which Isaiah speaks of as one of peace, joy, harmony, justice, love. And while we are considering these things, it might also be well to recall that this is a time of waiting and that all waiting requires patience—patience with ourselves and patience with others—for growth is never an easy or automatic thing. This four-week period, then, is a "sneak preview" of the wait still ahead for each of us.

But meanwhile, we have to listen to the John the Baptists in our midst—the prophets—who challenge us to prepare our hearts to welcome the Lord. And, perhaps just as important, we have to begin to look on ourselves as men and women who have likewise been commissioned as prophets, pointing out to others the same Jesus Who was long ago pointed out to us.

SECOND SUNDAY

YEAR C

Baruch 5:1–9
Psalms 126:1–2ab, 2cd–3, 4–5, 6
Philippians 1:4–6, 8–11
Luke 3:1–6

Luke begins his description of the ministry of John the Baptist with what must seem like a strange recital of even stranger names, and the reader might well ask what Luke's purpose of this all could be. The purpose was above all to show the historical circumstances that surrounded the Word spoken to John, and then also the world to which John would have to speak that Word. Luke is always intent on placing the Gospel into a definite historical context, thereby saying that the Word is never proclaimed in a void, but always in a unique, specific situation of men needing to hear that Word.

Today we meet John the Baptist, one of the more intriguing characters in the New Testament. Some Scripture commentators think that John belonged to a community of Jewish monks who lived in the desert, praying and preparing themselves for the coming of the Messiah. From what the Gospels tell us of John and his message, that theory is not far-fetched. As is true for many strong individuals, the reaction of the crowds to John was very divided: Some thought he was a prophet, and some thought he was a kook. Regardless of where one fell in those evaluations, however, everyone who heard him was required to take a stand on John and his teachings, and there can be no doubt that he captivated the popular imagination.

The Broadway musical (and later movie) *Godspell* (1973) opened with a song that took its inspiration from the very heart of John's message: *Prepare the way of the Lord.* If it is true that the Word of God is always spoken in specific situations, what is the message we might take here and now from John's preaching? How are we to prepare the Lord's way in this particular moment?

Jesus is coming, but He requires a certain environment in which to appear, one that you and I must begin to create—and not merely for the Christmas season. Therefore, our very first act must be a careful examination of conscience. The Opening Prayer for today's Mass asks the Lord to "remove the things that hinder us from receiving Christ with joy." What things are hindrances to your spiritual life? Are you a prisoner of your own desires and cravings? Have you become a victim of present-day materialism, unconcerned about the pain and poverty you see around you? Has God's law taken a back seat to peer pressure and public opinion in your life? All of these are hindrances to our reception of the Lord with joy, and they are considerations that call for our continued attention and vigilance. They are situations that demand a genuine change of heart.

And then there are other, special circumstances that exist only around this holiday time. How do these situations hinder us from experiencing the real joy of Christmas? While I would be the first to caution against becoming a Scrooge, I would equally warn against being sucked into that crass commercialism which tends to characterize the observance of Christmas today. In the hustle and bustle of holiday preparations, spend some time each day in private prayer and the reading of Scripture, especially passages from Isaiah, that prophet of the Messiah's coming. When shopping and in crowds, watch your behavior and check your attitudes to see if you are adequately reflecting the meaning of this season. Don't just go through the motions of gift-buying and card-writing; do these things with generosity and love, consciously imitating the love of God, Who set the example for us all by giving us the first and greatest Christmas Gift in history.

As today's John the Baptists, we must hear the Word of the Lord in our own particular circumstances and thus "prepare the way."

MONDAY

WEEK II

Isaiah 35:1–10
Psalms 85:8ab and 9, 10–11, 12–13
Luke 5:17–26

Earlier we reflected on God's initiative in establishing the Kingdom, but there is another side to that coin. We too have a role to play. People came to Jesus because He did astonishing things. Our task is to be other Christs who can attract people and lead them to the Lord. When was the last time someone praised God because of us? The basic question is: Have I been a good "PR" person for God? If not, now is the time to begin doing something about it.

TUESDAY

WEEK II

Isaiah 40:1–11
Psalms 96:1–2, 3 and 10ac, 11–12, 13
Matthew 18:12–14

One of the striking lessons the Sisters taught me in grammar school was that Christ would have died to save even a solitary human being. This was not pious speculation; it is at the very heart of the Gospel.

An essential ingredient of Christianity is hope—that virtue so tied to Advent—because we believe that we are in God's hands. No matter how bad things get, God "speaks tenderly" to us and will never allow us "to come to grief." The source of this hope is not wishful thinking but the coming of God to dwell among us as the Shepherd Who lived our life and was willing to risk His life for our sake.

WEDNESDAY

WEEK II

Isaiah 40:25–31
Psalms 103:1–2, 3–4, 8 and 10
Matthew 11:28–30

Today's Gospel reading, among the more "popular" in the New Testament, appeals to our desire to have a God Who functions like a super-effective Bayer aspirin. There are those among us who echo Isaiah's summary of ancient Israel's misperception: "God doesn't see my sins." Many go a step farther: "God doesn't care about my sins; He understands." Or even the foolish blasphemy: "I have no sins."

Jesus is indeed the Savior for those "who are weary and find life burdensome"; after all, that's the very meaning of His Name. However, being Savior, He saves us from the worst in the world and in ourselves—and that is sin. Unless we are willing to admit our complicity in the sin of the world, we will never know the joy of salvation promised in this season. The yoke and burden of following Christ consist in the forsaking of sin; only then is one able to lay claim to the gentleness of the Redeemer.

THURSDAY

WEEK II

Isaiah 41:13–20
Psalms 145:1 and 9, 10–11, 12–13ab
Matthew 11:11–15

In the not-so-distant past, it was fashionable to speak of having an identity crisis. For a believer, such an assertion is a scandal. Today's First Reading, with all the graphic language of prophecy, tells us who we are on our own: maggots, worms. Is that it? By no means, for with God's help we attain to a dignity unknown and unsurpassed, becoming God's special possession.

In His humanity, Jesus was a "success" because He knew Who He was and Who His Father was. Similarly, we should endeavor to know our human limitations but also how to transcend them. This ability is the first sign that we are really "Kingdom people," heirs of the Baptist, who could effectively point out the Messiah precisely because he had taken his identity from Him.

FRIDAY

WEEK II

Isaiah 48:17–19
Psalms 1:1–2, 3, 4 and 6
Matthew 11:16–19

The cynical proverb says, "You're damned if you do and damned if you don't." In much the same way, today's Gospel highlights the fact that if you are trying to please other people by your conduct, you are in for difficult times. Even Christ couldn't pull off that one!

The prophet urges his audience to heed God's commands (which may not please many), but such obedience does please *God*. This is true not only because we thus show ourselves to be His servants but because living according to the commandments brings us fulfillment—which is God's desire for all His children. That truth prompts Jesus to assert knowingly that "time will prove where wisdom lies." In short, our ultimate happiness is tied up with obedience to God's laws. How happy are you? Really happy?

SATURDAY

WEEK II

Sirach 48:1–3, 9–11
Psalms 80:1ac and 2b, 14–15, 17–18
Matthew 17:10–13

Today's readings focus on the future coming when Jesus will restore harmony to the world. We notice a certain calmness but likewise a note of judgment. Although Advent is a time of joy and hope, the reality of our lives also calls us to take stock of how we stand in God's sight.

Good religion is never easy; it requires balance, a most difficult posture to attain and maintain. Take some time today to see if you are despairing or presumptuous. The good Christian is neither—he or she is hopeful, which is a quality of balance, and that is directly related to harmony.

WEEK THREE OF

ADVENT

THIRD SUNDAY

YEAR A

Isaiah 35:1–6a, 10
Psalms 146:6c–7, 8–9a, 9bc–10
James 5:7–10
Matthew 11:2–11

Today is traditionally known as *Gaudete* Sunday, from the Latin word for "rejoice." The rose vestments and the frequent exhortations to rejoice remind us that Advent is half over and, better yet, that Christmas is only two weeks away. We rejoice, then, because we see our salvation is close at hand. In fact, Matthew would have us understand that the signs of our redemption are all around us. Surely, that is what Jesus meant when He told the Baptist's disciples to "go back and report to John what you hear and see."

If you read the Gospels carefully, you will notice that our Lord never spoke in vague generalities; His words were specific and concrete. He gave John's followers particular reasons for believing in His messiahship by showing how His works paralleled the works outlined by the prophet Isaiah.

So often we hear people say: "I could believe in Christ if He worked the same miracles today that He worked two thousand years ago." To this, I always respond, "He does—through His Church." In essence, Jesus gave as His calling card what we have named the corporal and spiritual works of mercy. Since the time of Christ, the Church has taken most seriously the obligation to continue these acts of Christian love as a sign to the world that Jesus is still among us, that His salvation is near to all who seek it. It is likewise important to make the point that the Church's works of mercy and evangelization will be only as effective as the commitment of each of her members. Therefore, if unbelievers do not see the Church as the place of salvation, the fault may well be ours.

There is also another problem. Some people—even within the Church—are looking for the wrong things and in the wrong places, as did the crowds in the time of John the Baptist and our Lord. They want the Church to be a social-services agency or a fuel-service station; they wish to receive everything from the Church, giving nothing in return. Or worse yet, they want a good feeling from religion, but not a challenge to their lives, which the Gospel is intended to be. As a result, they use the Church for their own purposes and brush her aside on other occasions. Like so many peoples' reactions to Christ, they find the Church a stumbling block rather than a means of salvation.

What can we do for such people? Well, first of all, I can tell you what we should not do: We must never change Christ's teachings to keep such people within the bounds of the Church. Jesus Himself invited people to leave His company rather than water down His doctrines, and we cannot do otherwise. However, we must endeavor to present the Christian message in as palatable a manner as possible. We must also share with these people what it means to have been "born into the Kingdom of God," to be a member of Christ's Church. People need to hear of the meaning and beauty we have known through our Christian faith. Be a contemporary John the Baptist for them by pointing them toward the Savior and His Church, for that is how anyone can "experience the joy of salvation," and that is the only real joy in life.

THIRD SUNDAY

YEAR B

Isaiah 61:1–2, 10–11
Isaiah 61:10b, Luke 1:46–48, 49–50, 53–54
1 Thessalonians 5:16–24
John 1:6–8, 19–28

Just beyond the half-way mark during Advent and Lent, the Church encourages her sons and daughters to rejoice. This day is traditionally known as *Gaudete* Sunday, from the Latin meaning "Rejoice!," which begins today's Second Reading.

The prophet Isaiah offered a perspective on joy for a believer in very human terms: The broken-hearted are healed; captives are freed; spouses are loved and desired by each other. As precious as those experiences can be, God offers even deeper reasons for a spirit of joy as He promises a world in which all people acknowledge His Kingship.

St. Paul goes so far as to say that a Christian must "rejoice always." Always? Even when the car dies and the roof caves in? Yes, because Paul says that rejoicing is "God's will for you." Christian joy is able to respond to the crises of life with confident assurance because it operates on the assumption that the real battle is over and done: Christ has conquered, and so have we. That's why we can "rejoice."

Beyond that, though, there is a very special kind of

joy, which is a gift so few people in our society possess. If I were to put it in Charlie Brown's language, I would say, "Joy is knowing who you are. Joy is knowing Who Christ is." That insight comes to us from the great prophet John the Baptist.

The Baptist was so effective in His work because he knew who he was and who he was not. You saw that so clearly brought out in his dialogue with the priests and Levites. One of the saddest developments in the Church in the United States over the past few decades has been a confusion of roles or a crisis in identity. We have all seen the foolishness of priests' wanting to run for public office, while lay people want to administer the sacraments. Religious masquerade as lay people, and married couples refuse to accept new life into their families.

With all the wonderful insights we have available to us from psychology, why do we have such confused people? One reason, and one reason alone: A failure to know Who Christ is. You see, we go about the process of gaining self-knowledge in the wrong way.

Knowing oneself does not necessarily lead to knowing Christ, but knowing Christ inevitably does lead to knowing oneself. How so? Because it is the Lord Who made us in His own image, and it is He Who gives us our identity; we do not fashion it for ourselves.

Our task, then, is to come to a knowledge of the one, "the strap of whose sandal I am not worthy to unfasten." We have the Scriptures; we have the Church to lead us to the knowledge of the Savior. So we are not left adrift in a sea of confusion. This sure knowledge of Christ and oneself produces genuine joy, which makes everything else pale into insignificance.

That is why we can be rather certain that, even as John the Baptist was losing his head to Herod, he was possessed of a joy that no man can take from us because it is given to us by Almighty God. It is the joy foretold by Isaiah; it is the joy commanded by Paul.

On this Third Sunday of Advent, therefore, the Opening Prayer of the Mass asks for the grace "to experience the joy of salvation," a salvation which comes from knowing who we are in the light of Who Christ is.

THIRD SUNDAY

YEAR C

Zephaniah 3:14–18a
Isaiah 12:2–3, 4bcde, 5–6
Philippians 4:4–7
Luke 3:10–18

This *Gaudete* Sunday, the Church presents us with a Gospel passage from St. Luke—often referred to as the "evangelist of joy." The text, however, is little more than a series of "do's" and "don't's." In point of fact, John the Baptist comes across as hardly more than a nay-sayer. A host of individuals approach him with obvious good will and a desire to learn and to please. He doesn't seem a bit impressed and then actually goes on to read them even more of a "riot act." Most fascinating of all, however, is that Luke ends this episode by saying: "So, with many other exhortations, he preached good news to the people." "Good news"? Really? Sounds pretty depressing, most would argue—but that would be only a surface analysis of the situation.

Zephaniah, you see, was able to preach a message of rejoicing because the people had already come to their senses—had already been brought to their senses through the humiliating and agonizing experience of the Exile, a punishment inflicted on them by Almighty God for their offenses against Him and His Law. The Baptist was trying to head off a disaster for his listeners by warning them in advance of the plan of life they had to follow if they expected ever to inherit the Kingdom. Doubtless, many considered him a Jewish Cassandra, full of negativity.

Interestingly enough, priests who preach "the full Gospel" of Jesus Christ, which necessarily involves talk about sin, repentance, and the possibility of hell, are often accused of being joyless and depressing because people in every age prefer to have their funny-bone tickled to having their consciences pricked. Ultimately, though, the genuine loving act is to confront ourselves and one another with the truth because, as Jesus reminded us, "the truth will make you free."

When someone goes to a doctor and says, "Now, Doc, if it's bad news, don't tell me," that person is not open to a true report. A good physician, however, will give the bad news (if need be), precisely to guarantee that something worse not occur or to ensure a return to full health. The conveyance of the bad news is the prelude to the possibility of good news, namely, the cure.

Is the application to ourselves too far-fetched? Do we want Christ, His Church, and her representatives to speak only what we want to hear—even if that puts our eternal salvation in jeopardy? Or are we mature enough to seek out "the truth, the whole truth and nothing but the truth"? Can we give ear to the message of present-day John the Baptists who challenge the presuppositions of our culture and thus invite us to that change of heart which will conform our minds and hearts to those of our Creator and Lord? Dante wrote: "In His will is our peace." In other words, seeing things from God's perspective and acting according to His promptings and grace are what bring us peace, which is but another name for joy. St. Paul obviously saw this connection, for he told the Christians in Philippi: "Rejoice in the Lord always. . . . And the peace of God, which passes all understanding, will keep your hearts and your minds in Christ Jesus."

Jesus' coming—in His Person and in His message—offer us true peace and lasting joy. Can we accept the former, so as to merit the latter?

MONDAY

WEEK III

Numbers 24:2–7, 15–17a
Psalms 25:4–5ab, 6 and 7bc, 8–9
Matthew 21:23–27

As we try to find Jesus in this age between His first and second comings, we should learn a lesson from the "religious" people of our Lord's day. Some were so sure they knew what the Messiah would do that they missed Him when He came. Sadly, many of them were asking questions not to learn the truth but only as a means of setting a trap; such people usually get caught in their own trap. Only those who are willing to follow an unknown star in honest searching can ever hope to find *the* Truth!

TUESDAY

WEEK III

Zephaniah 3:1–2, 9–13
Psalms 34:1–2, 5–6, 16–17, 18 and 22
Matthew 21:28–32

Do you feel uncomfortable when you read this Gospel passage? If so, it has the right effect. To enter the Kingdom, we must acknowledge our own unworthiness. If we *think* we are worthy, that is evidence that we are not. Jesus shook up His listeners by saying that sinners would inherit the Kingdom before the seemingly "religious" people of the day, not because there was merit in their sins but because they acknowledged their sinfulness and saw God as their only hope.

When Zephaniah (like the other prophets) extols the poor and suggests that they have a special place in the heart of God, he is not praising poverty or canonizing the lowly simply on that score. The poor are as liable to damnation as the rich who ignore them. Attitude, then, is the all-important factor—whether one is rich or poor, a sinner or a saint.

WEDNESDAY

WEEK III

Isaiah 45:6b–8, 18, 21b–25
Psalms 85:8ab and 9, 10–11, 12–13
Luke 7:19–23

Jesus' messiahship was not generally accepted, because His ideas were worlds apart from the ideas of the majority of those who heard them. He was a healer, while the people looked for a political activist. They did not understand that Jesus was calling for a much more radical solution to the world's problems—a solution that rests in the hearts of every one of us. Yes, God does "have a better idea."

THURSDAY

WEEK III

Isaiah 54:1–10
Psalms 30:1 and 3,4–5, 10–11a and 12b
Luke 7:24–30

The image of God we receive from today's First Reading is of a forgiving father who judges but then extends mercy. In a scene in the musical play *Godspell*, Jesus judges all humanity but then says, "Yes, you're sinners, but I love you anyway. Come on in." Now, we know that Christian doctrine does not allow us to accept that scenario, for those who die in the state of unrepented mortal sin are (by their own free decision) condemned to eternal separation from Almighty God.

However, there is a grain of truth in the scenario: God does indeed continue to love us even when we sin. And reflecting on that fact ought to move us to heartfelt repentance, causing us to respond to God out of love more than fear. And that is the real meaning of being "born into the Kingdom of God."

FRIDAY

WEEK III

Isaiah 56:1–3a, 6–8
Psalms 67:1–2, 4, 6–7
John 5:33–36

Hosea has been called the prophet of divine love. Today we hear him urge the Israelites to show that they know how to "return love with love." Jesus, the very incarnation of divine love, embodies this idea even more clearly, for love is also concrete, never nebulous. True love admits of genuine testing and never engages in game-playing or self-justifying techniques. At Advent's end—and at our life's end when Jesus' advent becomes real for us personally—will we be found loving?

WEEK FOUR OF

ADVENT

FOURTH SUNDAY

YEAR A

Isaiah 7:10–14
Psalms 24:1–2, 3–4ab, 5–6
Romans 1:1–7
Matthew 1:18–24

I am always amazed to hear of so-called "Bible-believing Christians" who refuse to accept the virginity of Mary, since it is so clearly stated in the Scriptures, as you heard today in both the First Reading and the Gospel. We know that the constant teaching of the Church is that Mary was a virgin before, during and after the birth of her Son. But what does that doctrine mean?

The virginity of Mary before and during the Messiah's birth points to the uniqueness of the Child that was born. Mary, responding to the call of the Father, was over-shadowed by the Holy Spirit, so that the Child to be born was both true God and true Man. His humanity came from His Mother; His divinity, from the Holy Spirit. This unique birth reminds us of what can happen when a human being cooperates with the divine plan.

Although the virginity of Mary after the birth of her divine Son is not explicitly taught in the Scriptures, we know that from the earliest times the Church invoked Mary as "ever-virgin." Why is her perpetual virginity so important? Because that aspect of the doctrine points to the uniqueness of Mary's vocation. She was not to be the mother of many sons but the mother of the one Son Who would Himself be the first-born of many brothers. Mary gave birth to Christ and, through Him, to the Church. Her physical maternity was extended to the Church by a spiritual maternity. Thus, Mary is the Mother of Christ but also, as Pope Paul VI spoke of her, Mother of the Church.

Our Lady was the first and best Christian for a variety of reasons, but two virtues make her an ideal person to emulate during Advent. She knew how to wait patiently for God to act in her life, and she was faithful to the Lord from the moment of the Annunciation to the moment of her Son's death on Calvary, right on through to the moment of the Spirit's Pentecost visit to the Church. Patient waiting and joyful fidelity characterized the holy ones among the Hebrew people as they looked for the Messiah's coming. A perfect daughter of Zion, Mary lived those same virtues. As our mother, she offers us her life as the exemplification of Advent virtues.

Mary the Virgin does not tell us that marriage, or the sexual expression of love in marriage, is bad. Not at all. Mary the Virgin shows us rather the uniqueness of the Christian vocation: that Christ is sufficient. Mary the Virgin shows us also the uniqueness of Christ: true God and true Man, worthy of our worship and our praise, Whom we now prepare to welcome as He comes to us in the Eucharist, just as He once came to us at Bethlehem.

FOURTH SUNDAY

YEAR B

2 Samuel 7:1–5, 8b–12, 14a, 16
Psalms 89:1–2, 3–4, 26 and 28
Romans 16:25–27
Luke 1:26–38

Advent is a time to think about giving God a home. Did you ever consider that God could need a home? In today's First Reading we see David interested in making a suitable dwelling place for the Lord. David knew that the Lord God didn't need a home for Himself, but the Israelites did need a place where they could encounter their God. And for his concern, David was rewarded with the Lord's promise of security for his dynasty.

In the New Testament, God actually did need a home, a mother, and a human life. Imagine that! This was not an easy situation, for many reasons. Mary was confused: "How can this be since I do not know man?" Mary was embarrassed, for she wasn't married, and yet she found herself pregnant. Mary was insecure, because the penalty for adultery among the Jews was that the woman should be stoned to death. But, in spite of all the questions, she said "yes" and agreed to give God a home. Through her cooperation, then, the greatest event in human history was able to occur. Perhaps that is why the angel greeted her with what appears to be, on first glance, inappropriate greetings: "Rejoice. Do not fear."

God asks us likewise to make a home for Jesus. That task is with us each day, but we think about it more as Christmas approaches. Making a dwelling place for the Lord in our lives is not easy; it wasn't easy for David or Mary. Like them, we experience doubt, confusion, and loneliness even as we attempt to make a home for the Lord in our lives. However, like them, too, we decide to cooperate, knowing that great things can happen if we cooperate with God's plans.

The Christmas season is a time of great hope, and so we are assured that, even though we are not always faithful, even though we fail, we still hope that we will follow the example of those who have gone before us in faith.

If we do, we are guaranteed that we will hear the same greeting that Mary heard in the midst of her confusion about giving God a home: "Rejoice! Do not fear!" Why? "The Lord is with you."

FOURTH SUNDAY

YEAR C

Micah 5:2–5a
Psalms 80:1ac and 2b, 14–15, 17–18
Hebrews 10:5–10
Luke 1:39–45

If you were God and had to find a suitable home for your Son, how would you select the proper environment and persons to be involved? If you're like most people, you might choose a royal family or at least one of substantial means and influence. You might search for the best city in the world, one offering the best possibilities for your Son's growth into manhood; no doubt, you would likewise want the finest section of that finest city. Selection of the parents would be crucial, and the joyful announcement of the birth would be made to everybody who was somebody.

Today's Scripture readings bring us into contact with some of the cast and scenery that formed a part of the drama of the birth of the Messiah. As we look at the situation, we might almost be tempted to think that God surely didn't take all that much trouble in trying to find the right home for His Son. But such a thought would be incorrect and shallow. God did expend much time and energy in His selection process; the difference is that He wasn't looking for the same things we might think important. We hear about that sleepy little backwater town

65

of Bethlehem. Poor, oppressed Jews provided the race, while a lowly carpenter and his wife were to give God's Son a home. The birth announcement invited ignorant, dusty shepherds to the baby's "shower."

As we hear these details today, we notice that they are more familiar to us as than the circumstances of our own births. These details make a point that we might tend to forget or overlook: God deliberately chose the time and place and persons for His Son's birth. The poverty and lowliness were no accident or unfortunate turn of events. No, God had this plan in mind from all eternity to illustrate that He loves and trusts most those who have the least, probably because they love and trust Him the most.

Throughout salvation history, it was God's poor and humble people—like Abraham and Ruth and most of the prophets—who pushed forward God's plan for mankind's redemption. These people were precious and indispensable precisely because of their firm trust in God. It may well be that this virtue of trust gives us a clue as to why Christmas so often means more to children than to their elders. The cynical and sophisticated people of Jesus' day missed out on the Messiah because they thought they had the details of His coming all worked out. However, the sincere and simple believers reaped a rich harvest. Like our Lady, they trusted that God's Word to them would be fulfilled.

In the days remaining to the Advent season, the Church would have us practice, with intensity, the virtues of trust, openness to others, and cooperation with

God's will and plan. Mary had prepared herself so well, at the time of the first Advent, that Elizabeth knew, almost intuitively, that the Lord was with her. Has our Advent been such that others will see Christ in us this Christmas?

DECEMBER 17

Genesis 49:2, 8–10
Psalms 72:1–2, 3–4ab, 7–8, 17
Matthew 1:1–17

Today's Gospel is not simply a list of strange names. Matthew wanted to make some important points. First, Jesus was a real son of David, with His ancestry going back to Abraham himself; He is a "Jew's Jew." Second, this Messiah has in his lineage a whole line of kings, but also sinners and Gentiles. Third, the genealogy includes the names of women (which was highly unusual in those days); this naturally prepared the way for the inclusion of the most important woman in history, the one last noted in this passage: the Blessed Virgin Mary, who was essential to the story, while the various men named were not.

This is Matthew's very charming way of saying that Jesus had a human history as well as a divine pre-existence; He was truly one of us. Far from being a mere listing, then, this genealogy is Matthew's way of declaring that the Messiah promised in Genesis is indeed for all people of all time.

DECEMBER 18

Jeremiah 23:5–8
Psalms 72:1–2, 12–13, 18–19
Matthew 1:18–24

The virginal conception of Jesus presents problems for people who are embarrassed by miracles, but a poet can understand (or at least appreciate) miracles, and one has said that "God works in mysterious ways his marvels to achieve." The conception of Jesus occurs in a unique way to emphasize the uniqueness of the Child to be born. At the same time, Mary and Joseph were not reduced to a passive role; their physical relations were not needed, but their obedience was. And it was precisely that obedience which gave God a human life and home.

DECEMBER 19

Judges 13:2–7, 24–25a
Psalms 71:3–4a, 5–6ab, 16–17
Luke 1:5–25

The Scriptures constantly remind us that a special mission requires special preparation, and this is brought out as we read of the conceptions of both Samuel and John the Baptist. The human beings involved in these events sensed the importance of the reality in which they participated—and acted accordingly.

We have been engaged in a period of preparation for nearly a month. Are we really prepared? If not, perhaps it is that we have failed to understand that our preparation is not for a one-day feast but for a life-long mission as heralds of the Kingdom.

DECEMBER 20

Isaiah 7:10–14
Psalms 24:1–2, 3–4ab, 5–6
Luke 1:26–38

A recurrent theme of the Advent liturgy is that "nothing is impossible with God." Hence, peace can become a reality; a virgin can conceive; the Kingdom can come. Although God takes the initiative, He requires human cooperation. Where would we be today if it weren't for all those wonderful Advent people—Elizabeth, Zechariah, John the Baptist, Mary, Joseph—all of whom said in their own way: "Let it be done to me as you say."

In a sense, God also goes through an Advent season with each of His children. Lovingly and patiently, He waits to hear us recite our *fiat*.

DECEMBER 21

Song of Songs 2:8–14 or *Zephaniah 3:14–18a*
Psalms 33:2–3, 11–12, 20–21
Luke 1:39–45

Today we encounter one of the more touching scenes in all of Scripture as the cousins John the Baptist and Jesus the Messiah meet each other for the first time, while still in their mothers' wombs.

Although the most hardened of persons down the centuries would find it difficult not to be moved by such a description, our contemporary culture of death reduces life in the womb to talk about embryos, fetuses, and protoplasm. The Author of Life will not be mocked, as "the former fetus," Jesus Christ, sits at the right hand of the Father to judge us for our complicity in the crime of abortion—either for our direct involvement, for our silence, or for our inaction.

Mary, Mother of the unborn, pray for us!

DECEMBER 22

1 Samuel 1:24–28
1 Samuel 2:1, 4–5, 6–7, 8abcd
Luke 1:46–56

Mary's *Magnificat* has probably inspired more musical compositions than any other New Testament text. How does it strike you?

Every time I pray this hymn of our Lady, I get goose bumps—because of its beauty, yes, but more so because I think of the kind of faith one needs in order to believe what it says: that God is great; that He is merciful; that the powerful have no advantage over the weak; that God is true to His promises.

The next step, then, is for me to pray for the faith of a child, so that I can believe that I am one of those descendants of Abraham who, like Mary, can "find joy in God my Savior."

DECEMBER 23

Malachi 3:1–4; 4:5–6
Psalms 25:4–5ab, 8–9, 10 and 14
Luke 1:57–66

The people in today's Gospel story are surprised that Zechariah would name his son John, for no one in the family had ever been given that name. This innovation prepares the way for that new age to be inaugurated by Jesus when many human traditions would be broken. As we learn from the Master: a man should love his enemies; the Sabbath should serve human purposes; external religious rites are worthless without interior conversion; divorce and remarriage are not a part of God's plan for man; and celibacy for the Kingdom is especially suited for the life of a disciple.

None of that, however, sounds like "the great and terrible day" that Malachi spoke of, but it serves as a prelude to it. Jesus' boldest break with human tradition was breaking the deadlock of alienation between God and man. That involved pain for Christ on Calvary, and our acceptance of that event's significance is painful for us as well. Just that way, we are able to approach the Lord with refined and purified hearts in the light of our restored relationship to the real divine tradition—begun by God Himself in Eden.

DECEMBER 24

2 Samuel 7:1–5, 8 b–11, 16
Psalms 89:1–2, 3–4, 26 and 28
Luke 1:67–79

Can Zechariah's *Benedictus*, praising God for the birth of his son, retain its hold on a society that looks upon children as intrusions and inconveniences? Can people who engage in artificial contraception, abortion, and child abuse (or who countenance them) truly appreciate the joy of Zechariah?

As Christians, we do not center our faith on a place or in a building (or any other material things, for that matter). No, the lesson of today's First Reading is precisely that God does not dwell in a house but does dwell in persons. That is why He became Man. That is why human life is so sacred. That is why each time we witness the miracle of birth, it is not foolish to see in it the birth of another child of God.